What Are Purple Elephants Good For?

From an idea by Tammy Cameron

Illustrated by Chuck Gammage and Steve Pilcher

Dominie Press, Inc.

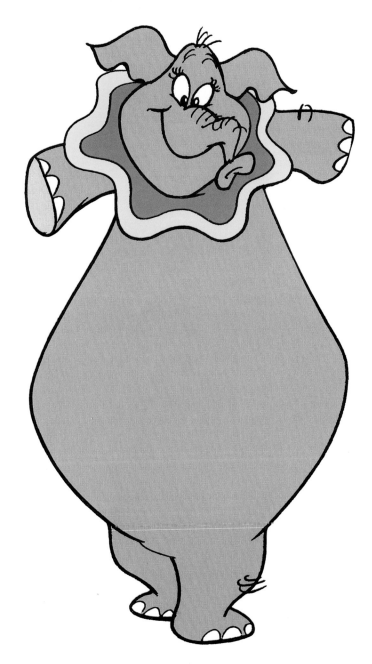

Purple elephants look different.

And they are very large.

But a purple elephant is good
for many things.

It can stop traffic if you want
to cross the street.

A purple elephant can make your room bigger.

And it's good at washing dishes.

A purple elephant can reach things
in high cupboards.

And it makes an excellent coat rack.

If you take a purple elephant to school,
it will keep all the bullies away.

And most purple elephants are
very good at games.

A purple elephant is good to take
on a camping trip.
It doesn't get lost in the woods.

And when you get tired, a purple elephant makes a good place to sleep.

Two purple elephants can hold
up your hammock for you.

Or turn your skipping rope.

And *three* purple elephants can...